That's a Good Idea!

Written by Jenny Feely

Series Consultant: Linda Hoyt

WorldWise
Content-based Learning

Contents

Chapter 1

There must be a
better way

4

Chapter 2

Where would we be without these?

6

Chapter 3
Our shrinking world

14

Chapter 4
I wish I'd thought of that!

16

Chapter 1

There must be a better way

An invention is a new idea or way of making or doing something. Inventions can be related to just about anything. They can be machines or food or furniture, or they can just be designs for things that no one has actually made yet.

People have always wanted to do things faster, more easily or more cheaply, so they have invented machines, tools, medicine, clothing and much more. Most things you use at home and at school were invented by someone. Some were invented thousands of years ago and have changed very little over time.

Others have changed slowly as people have **modified** them. Still other inventions have been around for only a short time.

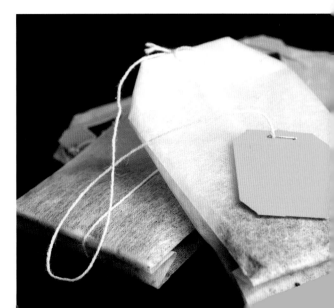

Discoveries are not inventions

A discovery is made when someone finds out something that no one has known before. Inventors often use discoveries to invent new things.

Did you know?

Paper was first made in Egypt 5,000 years ago from a plant called papyrus.

Zips were first invented in 1893.

Windshield wipers were invented by Mary Anderson in 1903.

Think about ...

Which things around you are inventions? How would your life be different if they hadn't been invented?

Chapter 2

Where would we be without these?

Many inventions have changed the way we live. Some have made small changes, but others have changed the world so much that it is difficult to imagine what our lives would be like without them.

The printing press

Then Before the printing press was invented, books were written out by hand. Only a few copies of a book were made because it took such a long time to make them. You had to be very rich to buy books.

After the printing press was invented, books could be made more quickly. But it still took weeks as only one page could be printed at a time.

Over time, printing became faster, with thousands of books being printed every day. Books became cheaper, and many people could afford them.

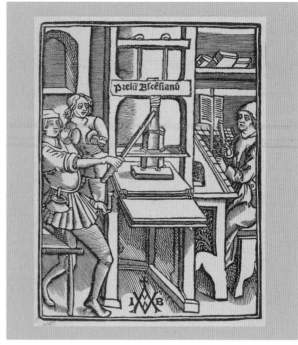

A printing press from 1511

Now Today, printing is being replaced by computers and the Internet. Some written material such as books and newspapers are published for screens instead of only being printed on paper.

The refrigerator

Then Before refrigerators were invented, people could only keep food cool using snow or ice. Many foods, such as milk and meat, go bad very quickly if they are not kept cool. In warm places keeping food fresh was very difficult. People had to eat food before it went bad, or preserve it by smoking or pickling it.

Now People can keep food in refrigerators, where it stays cool all the time. Food kept in a refrigerator will stay fresh for days. Food can also be frozen in a freezer and kept for months.

▲ Before electricity, domestic refrigerators had blocks of ice in the top to keep the food cold.

▲ A modern refrigerator and freezer

Did you know?

The first refrigerator was invented in 1748, but was used only by scientists. It wasn't until 1945 that refrigerators were made in large numbers in factories. This meant that many people could afford to buy one to have at home.

The electric light

Then Before electric lights were invented, people used fire, candles and lamps for light.

Now Today, people can light a room simply by flicking a switch. Lights are used for many things. They are found in phones, ovens and refrigerators, and are used to control traffic and to guide aeroplanes to the ground at night.

Melbourne lit up at night

The telephone

Then Before telephones were invented, people gave each other messages by talking face to face or by writing letters. Although letters could be sent a long way, it could take months for them to reach their destination.

The earliest phones had no dial. You had to call an operator to be connected to another phone.

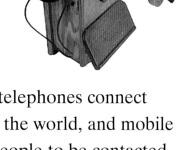

Now Today, telephones connect people all over the world, and mobile phones allow people to be contacted just about anywhere.

Today's mobile phone

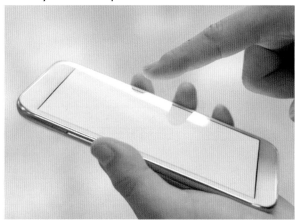

Photography

Then   Photographs record things so that people in the future can see what a person, place or event was like. In the past, the only way to get pictures was to have an artist draw or paint them. This took a long time, and only wealthy people could afford it.

Photographing a wedding, 1898

Now   Today, people use cameras to take photographs of anything that interests them. Photos can be printed on paper or shown on a computer screen or mobile phone.

Digital pictures can be taken on mobile phones; they can be sent to others to view on their screens.

Television

Then   Before television was invented people found out about what was happening in other parts of the world by reading newspapers or listening to radio. They were not able to see what was happening while it was happening.

TV set from the 1960s

Now   Today, people all over the world watch television every day. On television, people can see and hear things that are happening at the same time in other parts of the world.

Modern flat-screen display

Chapter 3

Our shrinking world

Bamboo raft

Viking longboat

Canoe

Once, the only way for people to get from one place to another was to walk. This took a lot of time and energy, so no one travelled very far. Then people started to invent ways of getting around that made it easier and faster to travel across the land and the sea. Today, people can travel from one side of the world to the other in about a day.

Getting around on water

People first learned to travel on water using boats more than 8,000 years ago. The earliest boats included rafts, canoes and **dugouts**. These boats floated with the current or were paddled or **poled** in the direction people wanted to go.

About 5,000 years ago, people started adding sails to boats. This made travelling over water much easier. About 1,100 years ago, boats were travelling across the ocean from one country to another.

In 1570, Ferdinand Magellan became the first person to sail around the world. The voyage took about three years.

Sailing ship, 1700s

Sail and steam ship, 1800s

Paddle steamer

Speedboat

Ocean liner

Container ship

Hovercraft

The problem with sailing boats was that they could move only when there was wind. But, in 1783, the paddle steamer was invented. Paddle steamers are boats that move through the water using a steam-powered engine to turn a huge paddle wheel. Boats never again had to depend only on the wind.

Over time, steam engines were replaced by other kinds of engines, making ships faster and safer. Today, people travel over water in many different kinds of boats. They can travel around the world in a few weeks.

Ancient Egyptian **chariot**

Steam train

Old farm wagon

Pioneers' covered wagon

Getting around on wheels

It is believed that the wheel was invented about 5,500 years ago. The first wheeled vehicles were pushed or pulled by humans, but soon horses, oxen and other animals were doing this work.

Wheeled vehicles such as carts and wagons made it easier for people to get from place to place and to move goods. Wheeled vehicles required tracks and roads, so people built these across the countryside.

Engines weren't invented until thousands of years later, in the 1700s.

Various types of engines were used to make trains, motorcycles, cars and other motorised means of transportation.

Now travel getting around on wheels was fast as well as easy.

Think about ...
How many ways are wheels used to move things? How has this invention affected your life?

Early steam tractor

Motorcycle

Modern train

Ford Model T, 1927

Early tramcar

Interstate bus

The first self-propelled road vehicle was a three-wheeled military tractor.

It was invented in 1769. It could only travel at about three kilometres per hour and had to stop every 10 minutes to build up steam before it could move on.

Although it was very slow, the tractor marked the beginning of many inventions that improved land vehicles.

In 1885, Karl Benz built the world's first practical car. Within 20 years, the Ford Motor Company was selling cars to people in many places. Over the past 100 years, cars have become faster and more comfortable. Today, people can travel more than 100 kilometres in less than an hour.

Think about ...
Traffic lights were in use long before cars were invented. The first traffic light was installed in London in 1868 to control traffic made up of pedestrians and horses pulling **buggies** or wagons.

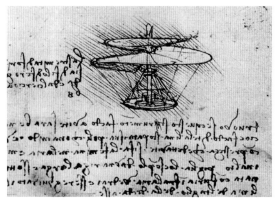
Da Vinci drawing for a helicopter

Air force jet

Hot-air balloon, 1800s

Early biplane

Getting around in the air

People have always dreamed of flying, but it was only about 500 years ago that the first real studies of flight were made by Leonardo da Vinci.

Many people who tried to make flying machines were inspired by his ideas, while many other people believed it was impossible.

Then, about 200 years ago, the first hot-air balloon was invented.

But hot-air balloons could go only where the wind pushed them, so flying from one place to another was difficult.

In 1899, Ferdinand von Zeppelin invented the first hot-air balloon propelled by an engine. It was called the zeppelin and could travel in any direction.

Think about ...
Today, we think of flying as a safe thing to do. How would people have felt about flying 100 years ago?

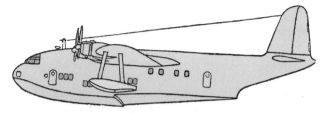
The 1940s flying boat could land on water.

Jet aeroplane

Modern recreational ballooning   Space shuttle launch   Moon walk

People continued to try different ways of travelling through the air. In 1903, the Wright brothers flew the first aeroplane with an engine. The flight lasted only 12 seconds, and the aircraft flew 90 metres.

Soon, planes were flying from town to town. At first, pilots needed to look out of their planes to spot landmarks to tell them where they were, or they followed roads. Then, instruments were invented that could tell pilots where they were, how high they were and how fast they were flying.

By the late 1940s, aeroplanes were regularly carrying paying passengers, and today, people can travel around the world in a day.

Think about ...
Today, people can fly into space. Is this a good idea? Would you go to space if you could? How far would you go?

The space shuttle
A space shuttle is a re-usable spacecraft designed to transport **astronauts** between Earth and a space station that **orbits** the earth.

Chapter 4

I wish I'd thought of that!

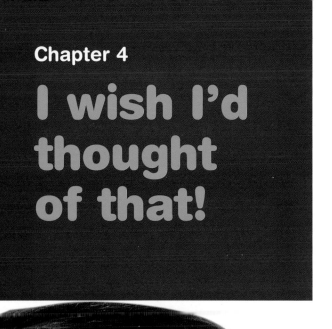

Bubble gum

Bubble gum was invented in 1906 by Frank Fleer of the Fleer Chewing Gum Company in Philadelphia, USA. He called his gum Blibber-Blubber, but it was never perfected.

Then, in 1928, the accountant at the chewing gum company, Walter Diemer, was testing chewing gum recipes and ended up accidentally inventing the first successful bubble gum. The pink gum was stretchy, but not too sticky. Diemer took a pile of his gum to a grocery store, and before the afternoon was over he had sold it all.

He then sold his idea to the company, which began manufacturing it under the name Dubble Bubble.

Did you know?

When bubble gum first went on the market, salespeople had to be trained how to blow bubbles!

12 October 1948

Hooked on you

The world of buttons, bows and zips is about to be turned upside down by an impressive new invention — Velcro. This clever product was invented by George de Mestral of Switzerland, who says he must share the honour with his dog.

Mr Mestral says he would never have invented the product if it hadn't been for the problem he encountered

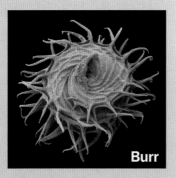

Burr

every time he took his dog for a walk in the woods. When they returned home, he always had to detach small **burrs** from his pants and from his dog's fur.

Wondering why the burrs were so good at sticking to things, Mestral studied them under a microscope and discovered they had tiny hooks that clung to the loops in the fabric of his pants. Mestral knew this idea could be turned into a great invention, and he set about finding a way to use it to make a new fastener. And so Velcro was invented.

Find out more

Where is Velcro used today?
What did it replace?
Has your life been improved by this invention?

Did you know?

Velcro is used in space missions because it is easy for astronauts wearing thick gloves to open and close.

Become an inventor!

Have you ever thought how great it would be to have an automatic bed maker, or a machine that picks clothes up off the floor? What are some unusual ways a rubber band could be used? Could you make a better pencil sharpener, or a better shoelace?

New inventions come about in many ways, but inventors often go through the steps shown here.

1. Getting an idea

Inventors get ideas in many ways, including:

- having a problem to solve

- thinking about how something can be improved

- finding a new use for something

- looking at things from a different point of view

- looking at how things happen in nature

- making a mistake.

2. Making a design drawing

Inventors often start by drawing their design on paper or on a computer. These drawings show how the inventor thinks her or his invention will work, what it will be made from and what it will do. Such drawings are called design drawings.

At this stage, some inventors take out a **patent** on their idea so that no one else can copy it without their permission.

3. Building a prototype

The first model of a new invention is called the prototype. A prototype is used as a model for making copies of an invention. Prototypes are tested to see how they work and changed if they need to be improved.

Continued on page 20

4. Producing the invention

A successful invention will go into production so that it can be sold to other people who want to use it. Inventors can produce their invention themselves or get other people to do this for them. A company that produces a person's invention pays the inventor a fee to use his or her idea.

Better bags
Margaret Knight worked at a paper bag factory when she invented a machine part that automatically folded and glued paper bags so that they had square bottoms. This made them much better for carrying groceries. In 1870 Knight founded the Eastern Paper Bag Company.

5. Marketing the product

A product can be sold only if other people know about it. People market their inventions by using advertisements, demonstrating how the product works at shopping centres or exhibitions, and even by giving away free samples.

Many inventions never get off the drawing board because they are too expensive, too impractical or because not enough people want them or know about them.

Tea bags

Tea bags were invented by a tea and coffee salesman named Thomas Sullivan around 1908. Sullivan packaged tea samples for his customers in small silk bags, and many customers brewed the tea in the bags rather than taking it out and putting it in a teapot. Later, tea bags were made from thin paper.

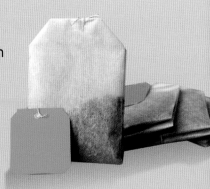

Amazing inventions of the 21st century

2001 Artificial heart

The first self-powered artificial heart was first used in 2001. This life-saving device can be used to replace a person's heart if it becomes diseased, without needing wires linked to external batteries.

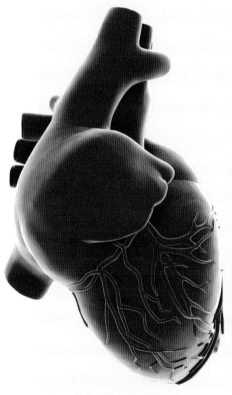

Model of artificial human heart

In 2002, the first robot vacuum cleaners went on sale.
These vacuums travel over the floor of a whole room vacuuming up dust and dirt. They even take themselves back to the power source when they run low on power.

In 2007, portable electronic books became available to the public.
These electronic devices can store and display hundreds of books in a device that fits easily into a handbag.

2012 Driverless car

Cars that do not need human drivers have been developed and have been successfully tested in real road situations.

Digital devices

The development of digital devices that can store and play music, photos and moving images has made taking entertainment with you wherever you go easy and practical.

Glossary

astronaut a person trained to travel in a spacecraft

buggy a small, light, one-horse carriage

burr rough, prickly case around the seeds of some plants

chariot an ancient horse-drawn vehicle with two wheels

dugout a boat made by hollowing out a log

modify to change, alter

orbit to circle around

patent a document from the government that declares the inventor the only one who can make or sell a particular invention

pole to push a boat through water using a pole

Viking a person of the seafaring people from northern Europe

Index